Magdalena

Magdalena

Maureen Gibbon

The Marie Alexander Poetry Series, Volume 10
Series Editor: Robert Alexander

WHITE PINE PRESS / BUFFALO, NEW YORK

WHITE PINE PRESS
P.O. Box 236
Buffalo, New York 14201

Acknowledgments:

"Un Bruit Qui Court," "Near Browning, Near the Sweet Grass Hills," and "Bells
for an Anonymous Child" all appeared in *Biggy's Candy Store*, an anthology pub-
lished by the Loft in Minneapolis.

"Un Bruit Qui Court" and "Trains Carrying Sleepers" appeared in *The Party
Train: A Collection of North American Prose Poetry*, published by New Rivers Press.

"I Call to My Desire" and a version of "Magdalena Remembering" appeared in
5 A.M., issue number 11.

Cover art copyright ©2007 by Susan Barton
(www.bartonartstudio.com). Used by permission.

Publication of this book was made possible by support from
Robert Alexander and with public funds from the
New York State Council on the Arts, a State Agency.

First Edition.

10-digit ISBN: 1-893996-83-2
13-digit ISBN: 978-1-893996-83-0

Printed and bound in the United States of America.

Library of Congress Control Number: 2007921243

Contents

Part I

Part II

For my kin

"The body itself is a dwelling place,
as the Anglo-Saxons knew in naming it
banhus (bonehouse) and *lichama* (bodyhome). . . ."
—Nancy Mairs

Part I

Un Bruit Qui Court

On the island, women are moored like boats.

In late summer the grass and ground vines of the island have dried. Crickets rub their wings together and all day long the brush on the side of the road ticks and scratches in the heat. Men have returned from the morning catch to sit at their dinners. Voices and the sound of knives and forks on plates come through the closed shutters of the island houses.

In the harbor the women wait. They are tied to logs sunken in the shore-bottom or to metal rings along the stone sea wall of the port. The paint on the boats is scorched, hot to the touch. It peels away in layers. These are small boats, skiffs, large enough for only one or two men. Fish swim beneath the boats in cool shadows.

The men do not understand that their women are moored boats. One side bakes and dries in the sun and the men know it is for carrying and ferrying, but the underside is a blue world they do not know how to see or harvest. Sometimes a plank of wood splits in one of the boats because of the heat. The sound is sharp, like a handclap, but has a small cry or screech in it, too. And there is the plank, split in two. The men can do that with their heat, make a woman cry out. She may also split silently so that you would never know.

Near Browning, Near the Sweet Grass Hills

It is the place I have always been going. Small white crosses mark the roadside, times a car passed over the line or lost its course. The crosses are sometimes called *descansos* or resting places, words less final than death. At one place in the road there are thirteen crosses, thirteen who have departed, thirteen journeys altered. The car pulls at me and I go fast there, too, say *I can handle it*. What the others thought. The washed out fields hold them now.

The crosses bless and warn that we sometimes love danger. In the north, the Sweet Grass Hills rise up out of the high plain and some ponies drink at a slate blue pond. Whatever it is that wants and wants – the sky is as big as that and keeps going.

On a Hutterite Farm

One by one geese are grabbed from the flock and turned upside down by women wearing gloves. The women snap each long neck into a collar that locks, the collars all part of a metal wheel. Children hover around this machine, so much like a ride on a playground. Above them all the sun shines. The offended geese sway in the wheel, each fat body pointing a bill toward the ground. Sometimes a goose may be reluctant to thrust its head into the collar. A woman leans close, tugs the head through the ring. Each wheel holds twenty geese. Three hundred more wait uneasily. Children disappear then, except for older girls who must learn things like this. The wheel is turned with a lever and a large blade shaves each head from its body, below the collar. No singing accompanies this work. It is not like pie making. A grade of dirt slopes away from the wheel and the waste from the geese gathers at its base. The tedious job is made efficient by a wheel, easier for the women. The geese express no opinion. Women straighten their aprons, sun high to the east.

The dolphins made me stay in that town. The first time I saw them I couldn't believe they swam so close to shore. The water darkened and blistered above the places they swam, and the strange blister of sea moved, ignoring the current. When the dolphins broke the surface, I could see their fins above the roiling water. On sunny mornings, the dolphins' bodies looked gray-blue against the silver surface of the ocean, but on cloud-filled days or in the evening, the dolphins were black arcs. When they left the shore, they headed toward the southern horizon, the coast of Africa. If I didn't see them on a certain day, I imagined that they stayed in some brighter water to feed.

I had a cheap room in the town, far from the water, in a *pension* near the train station. The coming and going of trains broke my sleep but comforted me, too. I liked to wake and think of all the people sleeping in their compartments, going further along the coast or north, and then I would sleep again. I didn't care that my room was small and that my sheets weren't changed every day — I was there for the sea. I walked to the beach every morning and did not go back to my room until night. In a week, my skin was brown and accustomed to the sun. I believe I could have stayed all day in the light, but always I left the beach at noon to buy fruit for my lunch and to find a quiet place to sleep in a park that overlooked the city. No one bothered my sleep, though they might have — a woman alone. My reddish-brown skin and tangled hair, my cheap clothes, even my smell since I bathed only in the sink in my room and at the showers on the beach — something protected me in my sleep. When I woke up, I went back down through the *vieille ville* to the beach for evening.

I lived like that for a month, then another month. I was too poor to go anywhere except the water, but I didn't care. At night I walked home along the avenue, my skin brown and tight, and watched people promenading in the night air. I could have had lovers — the owner of the *pension* knocked on my door with magazines in English and asked me not to call him *vous*, but I didn't want him. I didn't want the young Swedes who threw francs in my window when they saw me bathing, and I didn't want the young Arab workers on vacation from the industrial cities who hissed at my pale hair when they saw me walking on the boardwalk.

They were handsome enough, but I did not want a man. I wanted to sleep on my dusty sheets that smelled of my hair and skin, of baby oil, and the strange sea-sweet smell I carried between my legs. I lay in bed each night listening to the trains carrying their sleepers, and I thought of the dolphins. I longed to touch their blue-gray skin, and I wished for a tail strong enough to carry me through the dark sea. I wanted a body that did not split at the hip, that did not open and open.

I am afraid you will call to me from that world, voice thin and blue. I sleep, drugged, and dream a house for you: everything painted white and a row of windows looking out on fields. Lilacs, hyacinths and peonies prosper. Inside the house a book lies open where someone has been reading. Flowers in clear vases bloom everywhere, mirrors of the world outside.

At the end of the dream, it begins to snow in the fields outside your house. I never see you sleeping in a crib or on a child's small bed, but I know you are there. Everything grows quiet in the falling whiteness, a quiet I've never heard on this earth. I want to believe the dream means you are safe, that whoever was reading the book will care for you.

In my own body it is winter and beginning to snow.

Nuthatch is Gray

Each morning I heard them: a rush of wings outside the bedroom window, light click of feet on the feeder board, birds choosing seeds. I could sleep within the sound. I mean each time I heard wings and beaks, I could still sleep. It was a good sound to me. I liked remembering to put out seeds and was happy the birds were so close, that they came each morning to crack sunflower seeds in their beaks or against the tree.

I knew things then without seeing them: the nuthatch with his low whistle, squirrels that chattered and built a nest of leaves, the start of a steady rain.

I couldn't say why, but each morning cardinals woke me, a male and female. They came alone for a long time, then brought a gray child when they knew it was safe. Sometimes the male fed the female. Other times, both fed the child. Some mornings I lay in bed and watched them through the space between curtains, and some mornings I let myself sleep because I knew they would come again the next day. At the end there was always a whirring and clicking, then quiet. The female was brown but no less bold than red.

Klemencija Yuska

This summer when I lie down to sleep, I smell my grandmother's sweetness, old *muguet de bois* perfume. At first I think the smell comes from my quilt, but I sniff and sniff and know it's me. The smell comes from the skin on the hard bone of my chest where I press cologne, where the breasts and throat begin.

My grandmother is alive but so sick. I have her face and body, now her smell. My skin must mix with perfume the same way hers did, holding the scent and giving off something, too. The smell I knew as her all those years now mine.

Before the stroke she liked to write. Not about things — I mean she liked penmanship. She filled a shelf of speckled black notebooks with copied recipes, food she couldn't bring herself to cook. What she pushed from her mind as she wrote cups, teaspoons, sauté, I don't know. Her real words weren't for a page.

My grandmother never told anyone her Lithuanian name. I had to learn it years later when I read her autobiography, handwritten in a small, green stenographer's notebook. She kept her hair long even when she was old, wore lily of the valley, sweetest of perfumes.

Me, gardenia.

Work

It happened early on, my shaping. The first job picking pears that I hated because it was hard days of bending and carrying, always a weight around my neck or in my arms – and that I loved, because I could do the work, no matter how hard, and was proud.

I had to be careful in the way my fingers worked and held the fruit. I couldn't pull or tug pears but had to lift them gently, until the ball and socket joint broke. I picked fast with two hands and never looked down, slipping each pear by feel into a sack I wore strapped around my neck and waist. It wasn't only muscles working, but eyes looking for the next pear. I worked that job with all parts of me and sometimes there was nothing in me that wasn't used up by the work. Often I couldn't sleep for tiredness and cried over my legs, which couldn't relax. Some nights I fell asleep with the sun I worked under still in the sky.

Later I learned to want things that sweetened my life: books and paintings, languages and cities. They were sweet to want but they didn't change me. They did not shape me the way picking row after row of pear trees did, in the dew and under a high sun, or seeing the beauty of my own hands and arms, strong from all the lifting. All those years, and I still feel like that girl who worked hard, who worked hard all the time.

In Tall Pines I Hear the Mourning Dove

Years after I lived beside her, I remember her call. I know it was the sound she was born to, the same two notes over and over. Sometimes she cried for cold, for food. Other times just in song.

PART II

Magdalena Remembering

When I was young my body was money. I bought what I thought
would please me. I would have married a man who kissed the fine
fan of bones in my foot. I squandered my pretty breasts and thighs,
looking for him.

I never slept beside those men. I sat on their laps and pulled kiss-
es from their mouths – but I never did sleep. Never dreamed. I
couldn't let them see that in me: my pictures of red flowers, scent-
ed lakes, damask, orange trees. In dreams I breathed water. In
dreams I flew.

After a man left I'd stand a long time in front of the mirror, brush-
ing my hair. Thinking.

My belly's empty and I want something sweet.
My belly's empty and I want something salt.
My belly's empty and I want a bitter thing.

Somewhere there is a bird like my soul.

Interior, South Dakota

I cursed you those nights you called me to come and get you, drunk on the curb of Nicollet and 27th, there at the Tom Thumb. You'd hang your head like a kicked and half-blind dog, and like a dog, you'd whine first, sometimes cry.

Now it's me who needs getting. Six hundred miles from home and I had to quit this one, too. At least you brushed my hair, whispered *sweet* to my thighs. I want to call you up and say *come get me from this place*, the way you used to do, but then I remember who you are. A drunk who couldn't make it to my bed some nights. Then I don't call. I don't even pick up the phone.

November, Dreaming Deer

Fall and the woods are thin, snow on some of the branches. I dream a doe that night, her slow chewing, coat thickening for cold. She eats the buds and soft bark of trees. I keep listening for her words, but the dream is silent, only the soft sound of snow falling.

When I wake there are hunters in the motel parking lot. I watch them from the window. They are done with breakfast, they lean against their trucks. They talk in the morning air about her coat and her eyes. How the body gave way.

Chief Motel, Custer

I stand by the phone again but don't know a damn person to call. I go back to my rented room, the stranger waiting there.

It snows all that night in the Black Hills. When I wake up I see my clothes folded in a small pile. I'm glad someone is with me. He calls me "pretty one," holds me all night long.

Our Life in Martin

That one time in Martin we holed up in Harold's Motel, waited out the blizzard. Remember? The whole sky blew white across the plains. We drove out in the storm and you showed me the old rooming house where you grew up, the projects outside of town where you took care of your brother and sister. That night we even had drinks at the American Legion, you and me and all the ranchers.

That was a Thanksgiving blizzard but we ate microwave sandwiches from the convenience store. We didn't give a fuck. We were happy just to be together. I nearly got myself killed trying to get to you that time. I spun out on an icy road just outside of Mission and said a prayer when my car finally landed in a ditch, not in someone's headlights. I didn't have a god so I prayed to yours. I hope that was all right. Thank you grandfather, I said, thank you for my life which is good.

The fields were white around me, and quiet.

Deena and Elroy Three Scars came out onto the porch to greet you when we walked up to that bar in Martin. We all sat down in a booth and soon other people came and sat with us. People wanted to talk to you and none of them could believe you quit drinking.

"You found something to give it up for," a guy named C.J. said and meant me. I kept my arm around you. The whole booth was drunk except for us. I had a beer but you sat there with water.

Your brother used to be afraid every time he said goodbye to you. Those years you were drinking, he thought each time he saw you was the last. That's the way your father went: struck down on the side of the road. Closed casket. As if you'd know his face anyway, he stayed away so much. I think of that when we're lying in bed, think about the scars on your knuckles from bar fights and your stories of waking up in the tank. None of it killed you. You stayed alive long enough to live.

In the night the police come to the motel room next to ours. I try to hear what the voices are saying. When I tell you I'm scared, you say, "Go to sleep. I'm here." And I do fall asleep again, there with you in Martin.

Without Our Hands We Cannot Make

In darkness I used to walk the streets of a town in the middle of the country, thinking of all the land that surrounded me, hundreds of miles of earth, hundreds of miles of summer stretching further than I could imagine – where people sat on porches, drove highways, slept on cool sheets, talked quietly to children, danced in bars, listened to crickets, or walked, like me. Surrounded by dirt and summer darkness I thought I was safe in all that land. I thought it is america, it is america around me and nothing to hurt me.

Then I learned of her murder in winter. How a doctor cut away her hands. To identify her, it was said, but more likely to make sure it was over, her power ended. As if voiceless fingers could tell them anything. As if they could know her, ever.

Everything changed after I learned about her death. Some things I will not think again and some things I will always think. And I think often of her, when I am driving past the Wanblee turnoff, when I am writing or sewing or washing dishes or pushing my hair back from my face or touching someone. I wonder if her hands were returned to her. If she was buried with them.

That is what I think of now in the middle of the country.

I Tell My Back

My back, that old bone, misses his skin. His belly pressed up against her, breath on her nape. I tell her she needs to be alone for a while, that another will come.

Bones click when I lie down, then ache. *Where have you sent this one?* she asks. *You'd break me too, if I let you.*

Back Poem #2

A new one comes, in the time of sadness, when I am still trying to forget.

See? I say. He's kind, he touches you, makes it easier.

He's too young, she says. *A boy. You'll scare him with your stories.*

Back Poem #3

It turns out she is wrong.

The boy, who is my age, stays and stays. He burrows in my body,
likes to sleep in my arms.

It's not enough, she says. *What is soft is easy to love. I'm the test.*

Back Poem #4

I try to sleep in a quiet room. She wakes me. *I miss the big-bellied one,* she says, *the one who was so full against me.*

He's gone, I tell her. No one could love you. You're ugly and hard, a back of stones.

Look at my twin, she says. *Your heart, your heart, your heart.*

Their Slow Falling Dance

I drove ten hours then waited at the truck stop for your blue car. Thought about what I'd say to get you back: that we'd drive to Vegas if you wanted. I wouldn't let myself think about the times I admitted to any fault just to end the fight, or how you seemed to like me best when I was silent, not talking back. I told myself there wasn't anything I couldn't do or make myself feel.

When you got there you put one hand in my hair and the other on my black jeans. That's how we made up: on the side of the road. When we crossed the Badlands going seventy, we struck butterflies in the air. The windshield stopped their slow falling dance. *You're mine*, I thought. Monarchs flamed orange on the glass.

PART III

Guava Jelly

When I was twenty-eight I had a lover who spent hours touching my body. An hour on my breasts and longer between my legs. There was no place he wouldn't suck or slip a wet finger. After I met him, I wondered at how stupid I'd been all the years before, staying with men who wouldn't lick up into my vagina, the way I liked.

I liked what my lover did for my body but I had no real affection for him. I disliked his features and the scent of the oil he wore in his dark, waving hair. If he had been drinking, the whiskey taste of his mouth blended with his cologne so that he took on a pure alcohol smell. On those nights I let him kiss my body and put his penis into me, but I would not kiss his mouth and I did not let him into my bed. I didn't want his smell on my sheets.

When my lover came to see me we never talked long. I didn't tell him my dreams or read him my poems, and he never commented on the notebooks he saw on the tables and floor of my apartment. After a polite enough time, he would begin to take away my clothing, or I would stand in front of him and undress. Sometimes I answered the door in a corset, stockings and heels. I looked like a fleshy version of a centerfold, or a whore in some German movie. My lover told me he liked me because my heavy breasts and hips filled his hands, but he told me not to get any bigger.

Sometimes the way my lover touched me was frightening. I was not used to anyone attending to my body the way he did, or the utter focus he had. To him, my body was made to feel pleasure. Sometimes he insisted so harshly on my orgasms that I ended up with raw skin and a soreness that took a day or two to fade. My lover paid attention to me, but there I was, a thing again, just as I had been with all the others: a pair of breasts, a swollen bud, a hole. When I felt that way I told myself I wouldn't see him again.

Still, I couldn't forget some details. My lover knew how to tease me, whispering and kissing my panties in my wet cleft but refusing to strip me. He liked to study me and finger me under a bright, warm light. After a week of saying not again, I'd find myself wanting him. One Saturday morning after I'd given him up for the fifth or tenth time, I was driving down Hennepin and heard on the radio a reggae song with lines about guava jelly. I drank guava nectar in New York City a long time ago and the memory had nothing to do with my lover, but thinking of the small cans with their sweet juice — well, I couldn't call my lover soon enough after that song. Something in me wanted to be touched and I didn't care who did the touching. I wanted it done.

Home Through Town

Tonight when I walked along the river I heard a catbird. At first I didn't know it was a catbird. I heard a strange call coming from the trees and reeds ahead, a chirping with a funny *reow, reow* noise in it. I wondered what kind of bird could be making that call and then I just knew: catbird. I'd never heard one before, yet there was the word in my mind, ready when I needed it. I stood a long time listening to that call and watching swallows making crazy-eights over the water, dip diving for bugs. The wind was cold for May and sometimes it lifted them a little farther from the surface of the water than I figured they wanted to be.

I stayed along the water until I was cold through then walked home through town. I could have stopped for coffee but I knew I didn't want to be with people or feel their voices pressing in on me. I kept walking, but when I got to the door of the house, I didn't want to go in. I wanted to stay out in the night with all of its sounds and birds and callings.

I stood on the porch a long time thinking of that, thinking of the way I'd have to sleep with my arms wrapped tight around me, my body held small and turned in on itself, to keep warm on a night like this. I could have done it, too, but I thought of how much further a night outside would take me. So I put my hand on the door handle and I pushed down and I made myself come inside.

The Skin of Magdalena

Mornings I took my coffee at the counter with men. I listened to
their soft talk of the day, watched the way they kept to themselves
and the cup in front of them. I hadn't been with a man for a while
and sometimes I thought of touching one of them. On the hand
or arm. Nothing more. Mornings were for heavy cups, brown cof-
fee. At night when I brushed my hair in front of the window or lay
with a sheet over me — that's when longing came. I made a place for
it beside me, wrapped it in my hair.

Each morning I walked the streets of that town and forgot every
promise made to me. I started no talk at that counter, fell in love
only with flowers and the mountains behind Magdalena. I was in
my twenties and knew enough to let my eyes move over a man like
they did over a plain, a river.

Irene Sparrow was a farm girl who wore her dark hair in a long, thin braid. Some days her braid was neat and tight, and other days hair pulled from it in dirty strands. Every day of high school Irene wore that braid. She didn't let her hair fall loose until she had her baby. Graduation, her hair slipping loose, and her baby all happened at the same time. Her hair spread like a thin shawl across her back when she let it down, and sometimes strands caught around her neck. When the baby was old enough, he filled his hands with that hair.

An old man made Irene pregnant. He farmed the place next to her mom and dad's. People said he screwed Irene in his barn and told her it was a game. He got his old man's body up inside Irene before she even understood what he was doing, and he sweated his old-man sweat on her, there in the barn, like the two of them were animals. People thought it had to have happened that way because no regular man – no young man in high school, or just out of school and working in the Little Diamond mine or the mill – no young man would have wanted Irene, not with her country-stupidness and her homeliness. She dressed in high-water jeans and shift blouses, and she had a long white bone of a face that blushed low, almost on the jaw. Add bad graying teeth and eyebrows that were so heavy they met in a butterfly over her nose. When Irene got pregnant in high school, it was not because she was a tough girl who was ready and wanted a man of her own, and it was not because she was a sweet girl who made a mistake and tried to make the best of it. An old man had rooted up inside her in a barn and gave her a baby.

To the people who owned stores on Tulpehocken and sometimes saw her getting onto the school bus, and to the high school girls who laughed at her plain face, and to any of the boys her own age who somehow found themselves looking at her belly when she walked down the halls of the school — to them she was some kind of animal. They stared at her and under their eyes she was dumb and stupid the whole time. She went days without talking unless a teacher called on her and made her answer a question. What her life was like at home, no one could say. Yet her mother and father couldn't have paid much attention to her, because the old man was a neighbor and he screwed Irene in a barn that Irene's father could see every day.

What people in the town didn't know was what they couldn't imagine: that the old man was kind to Irene, that he gave Irene something she didn't get all day or all her life, that he wasn't too old to have narrow hips and a back that was strong from the work he did. When they were together in the barn it was warm, with just a little rain outside. And because Irene was so young and new, when the man started to touch her it was not without awe, so much so that when he saw her lying naked before him, he said *can I kiss it?* Even if Irene did not understand the words, the asking was good and sweet. She was there for the duration. "Can I kiss your flower?" was the way the old man said it every time after. Irene came to see that it was that way.

Vieille Ville

Traveling I had men in the cities, but when I went to the sea, I went alone. I burned each day by the Mediterranean, never sitting in the shelter of a cloth umbrella as older women did, but full in the sun. I let salt and wind lick oil from my skin, went deep into the sea even when the water rolled and turned me hard onto the beach. My skin turned the color of wild honey.

No one kissed me on the hot gray stones of Nice, no one walked beside me in Antibes where coolness seeped out of buildings and wrapped around my ankles. All the layers of my skin that had ever been touched dropped away.

George Thomas, Called Boone

I

I like talking to you without looking, our eyes on the river, floaters like moons. We always talk jobs and work but tonight you tell me about three Jackson winters you had the fortune to live. One colder than all others when you wrapped your feet in newspaper to gather wood. The winter you were sixteen and finally got to leave, north to Chicago. And just last winter when your father died. You made the long drive back and your mother and sisters were waiting: Lubertha, Angie, Shirley, Jesse, Clementine and Katie. You say their names over the water and I listen.

II

Driving here you told me you could see me leaning back in the seat, my hair blowing. The two of us going someplace, having a time. You told me you wanted to buy me a dress. I said no, I didn't want any gifts, then I said I liked to wear black.

Naw, you said. Blue. Blue is your color.

III

I see the whiskers when you bring it in: a small catfish breathing in your hand. So busy talking you almost let it get away. You take the mess of line and metal from the lip. I watch and want to ask: if I open my mouth will you take away what hurts?

The Way I Say Things

I get younger. The years keep falling away and I get close to the girl I was at seventeen. I knew things then. I made love on blankets on the ground and felt the night air on my skin where the boy's body didn't touch mine. I swam up under the waterfall at Sweet Arrow to stand in the space between water and rocks in the milky light. I walked railroad ties to a place by the canal where I could smoke and sit and sit. In the early spring mornings I walked down the steps in my father's house and let cool mountain air wrap around my ankles, beneath my nightgown. I thought nothing could take away what was cool and white within me.

Those years in the city I lost myself. I loved what was different from me: streets and subways, books and museums, Coney Island. Not that I'd give that time away, either – it's that I'm coming home now. Back to who I was and always will be, the way I say things good enough.

Some Are Green, Some Flower

Trees and flowers give off their smells in the heat like women, like I did that night. I stood talking to a stranger after the bar closed, let my dress lift in the summer air. I had been dancing and my sweat added its own salt and sweet to my perfume. My smell came to him on the air and he said *closer, step closer*.

When I walk past the park where he and I kissed, I look at the trees we stood under. I wonder if they remember me by my smell, inhale my scent, the way I do theirs, eyes closed. Some are green, some flower.

Dorsoduro

For the sake of the story, say it was the morning after you first kissed me.

I walked to the alimentari with Carol to buy tomatoes, the small bells that I liked to eat one after another, like cherries. I loved their sharp, red sweetness, loved them best when we bought them from the boats that stopped in the quarter.

Carol liked you too, so I couldn't tell her we had kissed. I kept thinking of that secret, and of certain words I knew. Anisetta, liquirizia, finnochio — seeds and oils that cleaned and then lingered on the tongue. The words felt good in my mouth, nestled on my tongue. I liked having them there against my lips, just as I liked to kiss the smooth skin of the bells before I bit —

I wanted to think of your kisses that day, and words the mouth remembered.

Sun Warmed the Bread

When I was in high school, I baked breads and cakes for my boyfriend. I slipped the loaves into Greg's truck when he was working day shift at Penn Dye. By the time he got off work, the tinfoil packages were warm from sitting in the sun. He thought I brought them straight from the oven, and sometimes I did, but most days sun warmed the bread.

I baked carrot cake, zucchini bread and banana bread, heavy loaves filled with fruit and vegetables. I wanted him to have something full to eat, something to put in his mouth and belly that would stay. If he ate as I ate —

He was the first boy I liked touching. We spent hours kissing by the falls at Sweet Arrow Lake or on a dirty bunk in a cabin. My body broke open for him and his for me. When we couldn't be together, I sent those moist, heavy breads, dense weaves of flour that were my body and my first lover's gifts.

I was sixteen and hungry all the time.

Who Have Been Told Their Gifts Were Not

—for Karen, Wayne and Elizabeth

We sat at the table until it was dark. No one rose to light a candle, to light the lights. We let the shadows come and let our faces become shadows. We let our hands touch the air, or our hearts, or hold themselves quiet in our laps. In the darkness we became voices. We each told a story, we each listened. We stayed at the table until we said all the words and ate all the words.

Black Strap

There is a small oily place on the bathroom mirror where I pressed my cheek. I had to lean forward and hold myself up on the sink to let you inside me. The basin was cold against my hands.

I wanted to see you touch me. Your hand slipped over the black strap at my shoulder, then under my hair. Your hand on my skin, your lips on my neck — I saw those things more than I felt them. So much wanting on my face. You looked up then and saw me watching. I didn't know if I could show you that part of me, so I shut my eyes.

I leave the spot on the mirror for a few days. I like seeing the cloudy silver when I brush my hair.

PART IV

In a Black Field

North of Blue Earth, Minnesota, in the almost-dark, I see horses in a black field. They bend their heads to touch mirrors on the ground. It takes me a long second to know the horses are drinking from ponds made silver, made fire, by the light.

I Put Aside Others

Each time I worry it will be the last time I have a lover. I worry that I will not find kisses I like. Someone to take my tongue on his, like fruit, like chocolate, like salt. I get small inside myself. The fear does that to me.

Then the new man comes and I like him. There is always something good and new in our lovemaking. Maybe he kisses my back or holds my legs to his chest. I let myself learn his ways and show him mine. It is never as hard as I think. I start to let myself walk slowly down the street again. I remember my beauty.

I Met Zeb on the Street

I could have had a job in New Mexico, started over, but I worried about being single in a small town, everyone knowing me as the teacher. I had a new boyfriend in Minneapolis, and I kept thinking of his dark hair, the way a small patch of skin at his throat jumped with his heartbeat. I could have found men in the new town, but I couldn't have been the same woman, taking home whom I wanted, taking what I wanted. I met Zeb on the street and let him walk with me until I liked him well enough to kiss. It doesn't sound like a reason to turn down a job, but I knew there'd be other nights I'd want to go walking, would want to see what the road brought me. If I find good kisses or a peaceful night in anyone's arms, it's mine to squander. I have to go someplace for my love, too.

Blue Dress

I look like my mother when I wear the dress. I don't know why I say that — there aren't any pictures of her in a cornflower blue dress with white dots, and it isn't the kind of dress she wore. Just saying *polka dots* makes me feel silly, but I feel beautiful and somehow womanly in the dress.

Maybe that's what it *is*: the dress makes me a woman I never thought I'd be, older and flirtatious, someone who wears stockings and rouge, who sits a long time at a kitchen table, drinking coffee and remembering. The dress bares so much of me — the shy skin at my shoulders, the light hair of my forearms, all the veins rising and crossing under the skin of my wrist. When I wear the dress, I can imagine my arms wrapped around a man's shoulders, my hands at the nape of his neck, my own waist tightly held. I think about the words *in my arms* and can almost feel it, as if the words themselves were touch, the way imagining brings feeling.

It's hard to explain what it means to see my own arms and hands change after so many years of being young. I remember touching the backs of my mother's hands when I was little. I thought they were cool beneath my fingers, smoother than my sticky girl's hands. "No," my mother said. "Your hands are softer. I used to nibble you when you were a baby, just to have your skin in my mouth."

My hands are beginning to look like hers. The veins show easily and my knuckles are starting to look bony. The skin doesn't give as much and seems thin. I know it means I'm aging, but it comforts me. It's like wearing my mother's old turquoise and pearl bracelet, or her engagement ring, reset with a blue stone for my birthday. Sometimes when I think of my mother I wonder how long she will live. My hands seem so small when I think of that.

Hyacinth

It can be winter, it can be winter and me sleeping alone, and that perfume is enough to change me. I do think of spring, I do think of the blue and white plants that flowered for Easter in my mother's garden — but the scent mostly makes me remember my life and the springs when I have loved someone. Each spring brought new hands touching my body. I rubbed the oil behind my ears, at my throat, between my breasts and legs. I wore the oil so a man would smell it and love to touch me, love to press his face to my skin.

The smell makes me think of wearing light cotton dresses, my skin cool in the spring air. Makes me think of showing my body to a man and waiting to feel him, wanting him to move inside me.

I smell the oil on my fingers now. It is January and I wore a little bit tonight for Ray. By spring I'll probably have a new lover. I'll wake up one rainy morning and he'll be here, I'll feel his body beside mine.

Touching My Scars

Once Richaux told me how it was hard having sex with me. He said, "When I touch you there, I can feel scars." I kept looking out the car windows after he said it.

In truth, I don't think he felt anything. He just wanted to shame me. He was the one who told me how he thought of my rape each time we had sex. The one who shoved a foot between my legs.

Now it's different. After my last surgery, when I couldn't bring myself to look, J. checked my incision every day. He described the stitches, the blood that finally slowed to a crawl.

And after the rough place healed, he kissed it.

Kicking Horse My True Husband

For so long I dreamed of union, my life wrapping with a man's. I looked for it each time I set out. Kicking Horse, Cimarron, White River — each gave me what they could. I found enough to go on looking.

Now in my dreams brown birds wrap themselves in my hair and otters weave silkily around my ankles. They hold still long enough for me to see the pin bite of light in their eyes, to see fur or feathers move over each heartbeat. The whole house scratches with their nests, their running.

Now even in love I keep a part of myself separate. The animals stay in my dreams and their hearts beat in each house I make. Their closeness, a kiss.

I Call to My Desire

I set out a plate for her as if for birds: sunflower seeds, raisins, a slice of apple. Grow morning glories, even in winter, because of the tendrils. All so she will stay with me. Sometimes my body wakes me from sleep and I welcome it, knowing it is her. Even if I don't have a man, even if it is all ache. My desire not less because I am alone. Her gifts. The taste of pears, salt. My body wet with its own happiness.

The Mountains Behind Magdalena

The house had a fireplace with one blue tile missing, windows that looked out on the dry mountains behind Magdalena. I walked the town and dreamed of fires in those clay rooms, fevers that would warm and break, evenings I'd spend watching the street. I thought it was my life and I filled my hands with it, greeting it.

To see that time now is to watch myself walking the streets, passing tin roofs, blue curbs, trees that spilled orange flowers like hair over stone walls and falling brick. In that town I passed things by, saying *you* and *you*. I let their lives touch me. The night I left even the air was a hand, a skin on mine.

About the Author

Maureen Gibbon is a graduate of Barnard College and the Iowa Writer's Workshop, where she was awarded a teaching/writing fellowship. Her poetry manuscript *Kicking Horse My True Husband* was a finalist in the Yale Series of Younger Poets and the National Poetry Series in 1994 and 1995. The author of a novel, *Swimming Sweet Arrow*, she received a Bush Artist Fellowship from the Bush Foundation in 2001 and The Loft Literary Center's McKnight Artist Fellowship in 1992 and 1999. Her writing has appeared in *The New York Times* and on nerve.com. She lives in northern Minnesota, where she teaches writing at Bemidji State University.

The Marie Alexander Poetry Series

Series Editor: Robert Alexander

Volume 4
Whatever Shines
Kathleen McGookey

Volume 3
Northern Latitudes
Lawrence Millman

Volume 2
Your Sun, Manny
Marie Harris

Volume 1
Traffic
Jack Anderson